Ripley® **Readers**

Learning to read. Reading to learn!

LEVEL ONE Sounding It Out Preschool–Kindergarten
For kids who know their alphabet and are starting to sound out words.

learning sight words • beginning reading • sounding out words

LEVEL TWO Reading with Help Preschool–Grade 1
For kids who know sight words and are learning to sound out new words.

expanding vocabulary • building confidence • sounding out bigger words

LEVEL THREE Independent Reading Grades 1–3
For kids who are beginning to read on their own.

introducing paragraphs • challenging vocabulary • reading for comprehension

LEVEL FOUR Chapters Grades 2–4
For confident readers who enjoy a mixture of images and story.

reading for learning • more complex content • feeding curiosity

Ripley Readers Designed to help kids build their reading skills and confidence at any level, this program offers a variety of fun, entertaining, and unbelievable topics to interest even the most reluctant readers. With stories and information that will spark their curiosity, each book will motivate them to start and keep reading.

PUBLISHING

Vice President, Licensing & Publishing Amanda Joiner
Editorial Manager Carrie Bolin

Editor Jordie R. Orlando
Writer Korynn Wible-Freels
Designer Mark Voss
Reprographics Bob Prohaska

Published by Ripley Publishing 2020

10 9 8 7 6 5 4 3 2 1

Copyright © 2020 Ripley Publishing

ISBN: 978-1-60991-340-3

Email: publishing@ripleys.com
www.ripleys.com/books
Manufactured in China in January 2020.

First Printing

Library of Congress Control Number:
2019954290

PUBLISHER'S NOTE
While every effort has been made to verify the accuracy of the entries in this book, the Publisher cannot be held responsible for any errors contained in the work. They would be glad to receive any information from readers.

For more information regarding permission, contact:
VP Licensing & Publishing
Ripley Entertainment Inc.
7576 Kingspointe Parkway, Suite 188
Orlando, Florida 32819

PHOTO CREDITS

Cover © Sergey Novikov/Shutterstock.com **3** © Sergey Novikov/Shutterstock.com **4-5** © Sergey Novikov/Shutterstock.com **6-7** © mTaira/Shutterstock.com **8-9** © JoeSAPhotos/Shutterstock.com **10-11** © matimix/Shutterstock.com **12-13** © lazyllama/Shutterstock.com **14-15** © Monkey Business Images/Shutterstock.com **16-17** © oneinchpunch/Shutterstock.com **18-19** © FamVeld/Shutterstock.com **20-21** © Gargantiopa/Shutterstock.com **22-23** © Melinda Nagy/Shutterstock.com **24-25** © gpointstudio/Shutterstock.com **26-27** © Dasha Petrenko/Shutterstock.com **28-29** Public Domain {{PD-USGov-NASA}} **30-31** © Sergey Novikov/Shutterstock.com **Master Graphics** © Anita Potter/Shutterstock.com; © vasosh/Shutterstock.com

℞ɪᴘʟᴇʏ Readers

Sports!

All true and unbelievable!

℞ɪᴘʟᴇʏ
PUBLISHING

a Jim Pattison Company

Sports are
fun to play!

It's baseball!

Will he get a home run?

The pitcher throws the ball fast.

It can go as fast as a car!

It's soccer!

Kick the ball in the net!

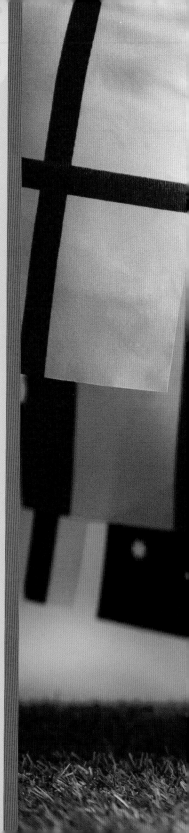

Some people
call soccer
"football."

Do you know how
to play basketball?

Throw the ball in the net!

He made a
slam dunk!

Tennis is fun!

Tennis balls used to be white.

Now they are yellow!

You must
run fast to
play football!

The Super Bowl is a big game.

More than 100 million
people watch it!

Can this girl
get her golf ball
in the hole?

It is so far away!

Did you know that there are
two golf balls on the Moon?

You can make new
friends in a sport.

Why not go out
and play one now?

Ripley Readers

LEVEL ONE
Sounding it out

All true and unbelievable!

Ready for More?

Ripley Readers feature unbelievable but true facts and stories!

 LEVEL ONE
Sounding it out

LEVEL TWO
Reading with help

LEVEL THREE
Independent reading

LEVEL FOUR
Chapters

Weather

Horses

Bizarre Buildings

Dinosaurs!

Baby Animals!

Trains!

Roller Coasters

Mummies

For more information about
Ripley's Believe It or Not!, go to www.ripleys.com